IN 31 DAYS YOU CAN CREATE SUCCESS IN YOUR LIFE BY DOING WHAT GOD DID IN CREATION

IN 31 DAYS YOU CAN CREATE SUCCESS IN YOUR LIFE BY DOING WHAT GOD DID IN CREATION

Hebrews 11:3
reveals that Worlds were framed
"by the WORD of GOD."

Rev Edward Johnson

authorHOUSE®

AuthorHouse™
1663 Liberty Drive
Bloomington, IN 47403
www.authorhouse.com
Phone: 1-800-839-8640

Published by AuthorHouse   04/12/2013

ISBN: 978-1-4817-4167-5 (sc)
ISBN: 978-1-4817-4166-8 (e)

Library of Congress Control Number: 2013906839

TABLE OF CONTENTS

INTRODUCTION

This is my introduction. I believe God wants mankind to have success and prosperity in his life. in this book, I will give bible proof of it. It's revealed to us in the scriptures. God wants to reveal Himself to mankind through a man or woman. When God gives man a revelation of what He did in creation, He reveals Himself to mankind. What did God do? Why can we do it? How can we do it? That what is this book is all about. When God created mankind, male and female, God bless them and told them to be fruitful and multiply. Remember God told them to do it. God did not say I AM going to do it. God said you do it. That's why God bless them. You may say how can they do it? God intended for them to do what He did in creation. We can create our own world by doing what God did in creation. When you read this book, along with your bible, you will have a revelation of haw you can create success and prosperity in your life. your life will be a true witness to others, your family, friends, even your enemies. You will the power of God working in your life, God will get the Glory when you tell them about the power of God working in your life. This is not theory live this way. This revelation is tried and proven, by me and others. M y ministry was going nowhere until I started doing things Gods way. Gods word work if you work it. We have been doing things the worlds way. and we have one failure after another. Gods word does not fail. God has bless us. The words bless means empowered to success. We have power to succeed doing things Gods way. In His word is His way. God bless you as you read.

P.S.

This book is for the spiritually mature, religious babies will choke on it.

CHAPTER 1

We Are Gods

This is chapter one. Genesis 2;7 and the Lord God formed man of the dust of the ground, and breathed into his nostrils the breath of life; and man became a living soul. Psaim82;6 I have said, you are gods; and all of you are children of the most High. St. John10; 34, 35. Jesus answered them, is it not written in your law, I said, you are gods? If He called them gods, unto whom the Word of God came, and the scripture cannot be broken. The bible records that in the beginning God created mankind in His own image, after our likeness. God is a spiritual being. So we are spiritual beings. That's the part of us that's like God. We are Gods children. Then we are gods. A dogs children is dogs,a cats children is cats, a bird children is birds. And God said everything after its kind. The first thing we must do is realize who we are. We may have low self image of our self. You are Gods child. God love you, more than your mother and father. Think about your mother's love for you. Its nowhere near Gods love for you. Gods love is unconditional for you. God paid the penalty for your sin, so you could always have right standing with Him. If you have children you know how much you love them them. You want the best for them. How much more your heavenly father? Children copy their parents. We see this even in the animal world. They will take their babies and teach the how to make it in life. How to walk, talk, fly, how to protect themselves from enemies? How to store food? The bible tells to watch the ant. If God put it in this, how much more His own children. God teach the same way. Take a look at creation in the beginning of the bible and see how God does things. How He created the world. As His child you can create your own world. God use words to create. Remember you are made in His image and likeness. The inner part of you is like God. God is a spirit being. We are a spirit being. First Thessalonians 5; 23. we are clothes in a body to operate here on earth. Our body is our earth suit that is the difference between us and God. Did you know a spirit never dies. We just lay down our earth suit, and go live with God forever. God wants us to live here now. We have a job to do here on earth. God wants every one of His children made in His image and likeness to be with Him forever. Some have rebel and are worshiping and serving false gods. There is a place for false gods and their children. don t go there. Follow the true and living God. Let God become your father here on earth. You be His child and operate like God on this earth. Only learn to operate His way. Copy your heavenly Father. His way is right. [rightness] lets look at 1ˢᵗ. thessalonians 5;23. And the very God of peace sanctify you wholly; and I pray God your whole spirit and soul and body be preserved blame less unto the coming of our Lord Jesus Christ. Notice the 3 parts of man spirit, soul and body. I say it this way, man is a spirit, he has a soul and lives in a body. The real you is a spirit. You have a soul, your mind, your will, your emotions. As I said before, your body is your earth suit. You only need it here on earth. It is good to know who you are, but we are not called gods here on earth. Lets read revelation 1; 5, 6 and from Jesus Christ, who is the faithful witness, and the first begotten of the dead, and the prince of the kings of the earth. [notice kings of the earth]. unto Him that loved us, and washed us from our sins in His own blood, and hath made us kings and priests unto God and His Father; to

Him be glory and dominion forever and ever, Amen. And now that we operate as king of the earth, kings have dominion or authority. So we have to go back to genesis to see where God gave man this authority from the beginning when He made man. Genesis 1;26,27,28. God said, let us make man in our image, after our likeness; and let them have dominion over the fish of the sea, and over the fowl of the air, and over the cattle, and over all the earth, and over every creeping thing that creepeth upon the earth. So God created man in His own image, in the image of God created he him; male and female created He them. And God blessed them, and God said into them, be fruitful and multiply, and replenish the earth, and subdue it; and have dominion over the fish of the sea, and over the fowl of the air, and over every living thing that moveth upon the earth. In these verses of scripture image is used 3 times and dominion is used twice. So these words are very important. Vines definition—image = representation and manifestation. Webster's definition—image = animitation or representation of a person or thing. My definition=represent a person or thing by first using your image, seeing yourself as that person or with that thing or things. That's how you begin calling those things that be not as through they were as GOD taught Abraham the father of faith. That's how GOD uses His faith. We are His children, we should imitate Him. GOD name it and claim it in creation. This is how GOD created His world. This is how we create our world. I believe you can do it in 30 days. It may take some longer because of much unbelief in you. Remember what the man said to JESUS, I believe, help my unbelief. Let's look at definition of dominion. As a noun= force, strength, might, manifested power. It's important to manifest power. The definition as a verb to be lord overrule over, have dominion over. When Satan was talking to eve in the garden, in Genesis 3, remeber GOD had told Adam in Genesis 2:15 to keep the garden, which means guard it. When I was in the army I had guard duty about 2 or 3 o'clock in the morning. To watch while other solders slept to keep away the enemy. This is what Adam was supposed to do when his wife was talking to the devil. He was to rule over, lord over his wife, tell her not to talk to the devil and with dominion which means authority, tell the devil to go and with manifested power of his words, resisting the devil, Satan would have flee in terror. And chapter 3 in Genesis, would never have been written in the bible. Chapter 4 would have been different, because death would not have been introduced into the world. Cain would not have kill Abel he would have love his brother and God would have forgiven him. and they all would have touch the tree of life and live forever.

CHAPTER 2

As Kings and Priests on Earth

Revelation1:5, 6. And from Jesus Christ, who is the faithful witness, and the first begotten of the dead, and the prince of the kings of the earth. Into Him that love us, and washed us from our sins in His own blood and hath made us kings priests unto GOD and His Father; to Him be glory and dominion forever and ever. Amen. Romans 5:17 for if by one man's offence death reigned by one: JESUS CHRIST.kjv. Amplified bible, Romans 5:17 reads for if because of one man's trespass death reigned through that one, much more surely will those who receive GOD'S over flowing grace unmerited favor and the free gift of righteousness [putting them into right standing with Himself.]reign as kings in life through one man JESUS CHRIST. [the MESSIAH, the Anointed One] we have the two or three witness establishing this truth we are kings and priests. Let's look at the word reign in Webster's new world dictionary, reign; to rule, royal power, authority. Vines dictionary of New Testament words of believers shall reign in life indicates the activity of life in fellowship with Christ in His sovereign power, reaching its fullness here after. So we concluded reign means rule, having authority, royal power, sovereign power. This is what Adam and eve gave Satan in the garden of Eden, so by one man's offence death reigned. But we must keep reading the verse, much more we which receive abundance of grace and the gift of rightness shall reign in life by JESUS CHRIST, the second Adam. What Adam loss, JESUS got it all back. Our redemption so we born again believers can rule in life having authority. We are kings. What do kings do? Declare and decree is the answer. Less go back to genesis one and two chapters. Everything Adam and eve lost in the garden JESUS got it back. So forget genesis three. That makes Satan mad, he is a defeated foe, and knowing it. I ask the question? Do you and I know it. That's why I am writing this book. GOD wants us to know, we have the victory through His Son Lord JESUS. So now let's reign in life. What did Adam originally do to reign in life. He copied his father GOD. Let's read Ephesians 5:1 kings James bible and amplified. Be ye therefore followers of GOD, as dear children: that was KJ bible. Now lets read amplified bible. Be imitators of GOD. [copy HIM and follow His example]. as well beloved children [imitate their father]. in creation after the spirit of GOD moved upon the face of the waters GOD said let there be light and there was light. And followed with 8 [and GOD said]. why did not the bible say one, and GOD said, and list all 9 saying. I believe the word of God or GOD want us to see the important of words. Words are the way we use our dominion or authority, the way we rule or reign in life, causing success. Notice genesis 2:20 Adam using his authority give names to all cattle and to the fowls of the air, and to every beast of the field: this brings us to the important of words, in ruling and reigning in life. To be successful in life you must use your words alright. using words wrong will cause failure in life. The scripture o back this up is first part of proverbs 18:21. death and life are in the power of the tongue. Again the dominate words you use in life will success or failure. Dominate come from the word dominion, what GOD gave Adam in Genesis one. How do words have dominion or authority? Go to the New Testament, Romans 10:8-10. these verses of scripture describe how you receive salvation. Receiving JESUS

CHRIST in your life, so you can reign with Him here on the earth. This is where it begins. It starts right here, you begin to reign in life. Lord JESUS died for your sin, past, present, and future. When GOD raises Jesus from the dead you and I was risen with Him. And Satan did to Adam was wipe out forever. We believers have eternal life, meaning living forever for a time here on the earth, then with the Father in heaven. Believe this gives you power on earth.

CHAPTER 3

The Importance of Words, God's Word and Your Words In Your Heart

Confession brings Possession why confess God's word? Words are important. God's word and our words. Remember words are the way we use our authority in the earth. But we need to speak in line with God's word. The devil will bring thoughts to your mind. But don't say them. Second Corinthians 10;5 says casting down imaginations and every high thing that exalteth itself against the knowledge of God, and bring in captivity ever thought to the obedience of Christ. I underline every thought. That's important. The devil may bring it, but don't you speak it. In Matthew 6; 31 Lord Jesus said you take a though by saying it. So don't say those thoughts the devil bring to your mind. You cast that thought down by saying something from the word of God. And thinking that thought your thoughts will influence the words you say. I am writing about the important of words, God's word and your words. Spoken words are powerful. They create good are bad in your life. Let's look at St. John 6; 63 KJV. And amplified bible. It is the Spirit that quickeneth; the flesh profiteth nothing. The words that I speak unto you, they are spirit. And they are life. It is the Spirit who gives life. [He is the life-giver];the flesh conveys no benefit whatever.[there is no profit in it]. the words [truths] that I have been speaking to you are spirit and life. The first thing I want to say about these verses of scripture is the thoughts Satan put in your mind is flesh or natural, not spiritual so they profit nothing but fear and doubt. Remember John 10:10 say Satan is a thief that comes to steal, kill, and destroy. Lord Jesus said I AM come that you have life abundantly. Satan is for death [failure]lord Jesus is for life[success]. now let me teach about what Jesus is saying in John 6:63 and we will see the important of words, our words and God's word. God's spirit gives life. His words are Spirit. Satan spirit gives death. Satan's words are spirit but come from the flesh. Flesh words do not produce everlasting success. Now we see life and death the power of the tongue again. Proverbs 18:21. look at ST. John1:1 in the beginning was the word, and the word was with GOD and the word was GOD. The word with GOD, the word was GOD. Go down to verse 14 same chapter. The anointed word became flesh. That's Lord JESUS. So when we receive Him, we reign or rule with Him. Represent Him on the earth by speaking His word. His Word is anointed. Our words become anointed by speaking His Word only. Christ means anointed one, not His last name. Now we see the important of our words speaking His words. Jesus' words are anointed and eternal, everlasting not temporal and death bound like Satan. "From our Heart" to give life God's word has to come from our heart not just our head. We read the bible or hear a minister preach or teach. That's just information in our head. But when we hear and hear the word, faith comes in that word and dwell in our heart. When that happens the word in your heart becomes powerful. And you speak it out of your mouth, it creates and cause what you are saying to come to pass. The devil uses this same power to bring his will in your life to pass. Fear then failure. This is how he steals, kills, and destroys. This is why it is very important what we say especially during test, trials, and tribulations. Those words come to pass. Born Again' this all begins when we get born again. So let's go to Romans 0:8, 9,10. remember this first happen in Genesis1:26,27,28. and genesis2:7. born into life.[spirit, soul and body]. this happen then, Adam lose it but Lord Jesus got it back.[i am emotional 'hallelujah, praise the Lord."] but what saith it? The word is near thee, even in thy mouth and in thy heart; that is, the word of faith, which we preach; that if thou shall confess with thy mouth the Lord Jesus and shall believe in thine heart that GOD hath raised Him from the dead. You shall be saved for with the heart man believeth into righteousness: and with the mouth confession is made into salvation. These scriptures tell us how to get born again. The word must be in your heart and spoken out of your mouth. That Jesus died for your sins and GOD raise Him from the dead. Let's read verse 10 from the amplified bible. For with the heart a person believes and with the mouth he confesses openly and speaks out freely his faith and confirms his salvation, he is born again. He had to be born again because of what Adam lost. Jesus said in St. John 3:3

except a man be born again he cannot see the kingdom of God. So now that we have our authority back, we can reign and rule in our life. We do this by our words. St. Matthew 12:34, 35 said for out of the abundance of the heart the mouth speaketh. A good man out of the good treasure of the heart bringeth forth good things and an evil man bringeth forth evil things. Things are brought forth speaking from the heart, good are bad. So we must watch what we say from our heart. How do we get it in our heart? What you continue say over and over will get in your heart. And when you speak it out of your mouth it will eventually come to pass in your life. This brings us to the important of confessing God's word. Remember the word was with God, and the word was God; so you won't God's word to come to pass in your life. God's woed is spirit and life. God's words will cause you to have success in life. Fear filled words coming from the devil will defeat you. Words are must powerful. Again watch what you say. Joshua 1:8 and Psalms1:1-3 is another way to get God's word in our heart so we can speak it out of our mouth. This book of the law shall not depart out of thy mouth; but thou shall meditate therein day and night. That thou mayest observe to do according to all that is written therein, for then thou shall make thy way prosperous and then thou shall have good success.KJV. And now amplified bible versions; only last sentence. For then you shall make your make your way prosperous and then you shall deal wisely and have good success. The amplified bible reads like this; Bless is the man who walks and lives not in the counsel of the ungodly following their advice, their plans and purposes or stands in the path where sinner walk, or sits down where the scornful gather. But his delight and desire are in the word of the Lord, the precepts, the instruction, the teaching of God he habitually meditate ponders and studies by day and by night. And he shall be like a tree firmly planted by the streams of water, ready to bring forth its fruit in its season its leaf also shall not fade or wither and everything he does shall prosper. God told Joshua to meditate his word day and night, meaning all the time. He would prosper and have good success in life and leading God's people. Psalm 1:1 starts off with the word Bless meaning empower to prosper. And not walking in ungodly counsel. But delight and desire counsel from meditating God's word day and night. Again all the time, He would be like a tree planted by the rivers of water bringing forth fruit in season. In other words, if he did this everything he does would prosper and would have success in life. The word meditate means to study, to think deeply, continue thought, mutter to oneself. What you are doing is getting God's word in your heart. Remember God's word is spirit and life. St. John 6:63. and St. John 1:1 the word was with God and the word was God. After meditating the word, you speak it out of your mouth continually, you get the same result God did when He created the world. Now you create your world. "Praise

God." More information on the important of words, God's word: My son attends to my words: submit to my saying. Let them not depart from you sight: keep them in the center of your heart. They are life to those who find them. Healing and health to all their flesh. Keep and guard your heart with all diligence; for out of it are the issues of life. Put away from you false and dishonest speech and willful and contrary talk. Put far from you. Proverbs 4:20-24 now your words: you are snared with the words of your mouth. You are caught and are taken with take words of thy mouth. Proverbs6:2. In these scripture from proverbs look the important of God's word and your words. We need to read God's word and be a doer of God's word. Daily keep God's word in our sight so it will be in the center of our heart. Remember God's word is life and spirit. And can cause healing and health in your body. You've got to guard your heart from worldly things that's of the devil. Because from your heart comes the issues of life good or bad, life or death, from God's word or the devil's deception. He is still doing what he did to Adam and Eve. Watch what you partake of. Again guard your heart verse 24 is talking about watch what you say which brings us to Proverbs 6:2 your words. You are snared taken, caught by the words of your mouth. Be very careful what you say during times of your faith being tested thru trials, tribulations. Pass the test or you will take it over again. The devil will see to it.[smile] Psalm 119;105 says God's word is a light to our path. Verse 130 of the same chapter says the entrance and unfolding of God's word light. There you have it the important of God's word and our words. Next chapter we are going to talk about sight.

CHAPTER 4

Seeing both Natural and Spiritual

Watch what you see. What you see is also important. In genesis3:6 when the woman SAW that the tree was good for food, and that it was pleasant to the eyes; etc. The devil deceives herby what she saw that was pleasant to her eyes. A person can be deceived by the things of this world. You must watch what is pleasant to your eyes. The same deceiver is loose in the earth, seeking whom he may devour. Psalm 119 says the word gives light to our path. That whole chapter should be read by every believer who wants success in life. Proverbs 4:21 and 25 let them [my words] not depart from thine EYES: keep them [my word] in the midst of thine heart. Let your eyes look right on [with fix purpose]let your gaze be strait before you. AMP. This brings us to meditation. Meditation also causes us to SEE on the inside, in your heart or spirit. Eve began to meditate on that tree. She was and we are a spirit being. What you meditate on, remember as he thinks in his or her heart so is he. Proverbs 23:7A. That's why 2Corinthians 10:5 tells us casting down imaginations, and everything that exalteth himself against the knowledge of God and bringing into captivity every thought to the obedience of Christ. [the word]. Joshua 1:8 and Psalm 1:2 says we should meditate God's word day and night to prosper and have good success in life, our daily life. Meditation is seeing. Imagination is seeing. We can get some firsthand information about the power of imagination

Philippians 2:5 says let this mind be in you which was also in Christ Jesus. If we are going to reign or rule in life and have dominion we must think like He thinks, which is God thoughts. We get God thoughts from His word. His word will not return void.[without producing any effect]. AMP. Isaiah 55:11 Look like I am getting back to words, but your thoughts effect your words. The angels or listening when you voice God's word. They take it as a command coming from God. Psalm 103:20. Read it for yourself. Well I have given you a lot about the important of thoughts and words. Next chapter will be about power and authority.

CHAPTER 5

Power and Authority

So God gave His man [Adam] dominion which is authority. Adam lose it. Genesis 3:6. But Jesus was the last Adam. 1Corinthians 15:45-47. The first man Adam was made a living soul; the last Adam was made a quickening spirit. The amplified bible says a life giving spirit.[restoring the dead to life]. So we have our life and authority back thru Jesus the second Adam. We were dead because of Adam's sin. Made alive because of Jesus rightness. 2Corinthians 5:21. He hath made Him to be sin for us, who know sin, that we might be made the righteousness of God in Jesus the Christ. The Anointed one. A second witness establishing this truth. Romans 5:17 For if by one's offence death reign gy one [adam] much more they which receive [us[abundance of grace [unmerited favor] the free gift of rightness [AMP] putting them into right standing with God] reign as Kings in life through the one man Jesus Christ [the Messiah the Anointed one]. So we have power to rule in life to create our success in life. The execution of that authority. St. John 16:23. In that day you shall ask me nothing. I say into you, whatsoever you shall ask the Father [God]in my name, He will give it you. There is another witness of your authority. Matthew28:18,19a. Jesus said all power is given unto me in heaven and in earth. Go you therefore. He is given us power and authority to reign or rule in life as kings. Remember you are gods[small g]. God's children.[smile PTL]. 1

John4:4b greater is He that is in you, than he that is in the world. God's image and likeness in you. Ephesians tell us about this power that's in us. 1:19. In Ephesians 1 and 3 the Apostle Paul prayer for the people of God who had faith in the Lord Jesus and love for one another that they would receive a spirit of wisdom and revelation, that the eyes of their heart be flooded with light. So they would know the hope of God's calling and the richness of His glorious inheritance in the saints[His sep aport ones]. The people who put their faith in the Lord Jesus and love for one another, so they can know and understand the exceeding greatness of His power to the believer. The same mighty power which He demonstrated in Christ when He raise Him from the dead and set Him at His own right hand in the heavenly places. Suggest you read these prayers from your bible, meditate them and receive a spirit of wisdom and revelation as the Ephesians did. You must pray also that the Holy Spirit will give it to you. We are the body of

Christ in the earth today, anointed ones. And all things of the devil is under our feet. We have the authority and power to put Satan and his works under our feet. Let's look at Paul's prayer chapter 3:14-21. Again our need to take time and carefully read and meditate this prayer. It's important to the believer. Paul took time and bow on his knees into the Father of our Lord Jesus Christ, of whom every family in heaven and earth is name, that we would be strengthened with might by His Spirit in our inner man.[inside of us] our spirit. And since Christ is in our heart by faith we are rooted and grounded in love. We must experience the breadth and length and depth and height of it. When you experience it you have more than mere knowledge of it. This is so you can be filled with the fullness of God. I will talk about the importance of this love in later chapter of this book. These last two verses of the prayer are very important to the body of Christ. We must understand verse 20. Verse 20 of eph.3. says because of God's power that's in us or the action of that power God is able to do exceeding abundantly above all that we ask or think. If our thinking is too low, our asking is too low. We must ask according to God's ability not ours. Sometimes we ask according to our ability to do something. We think I don't have the money to do what God is telling me to do. If God is telling us to do something according to His word, remember Philippians' 4:19 My God shall supply all my needs according to His riches in glory by Christ Jesus. God said to me, son your thinking is too low, If I Bless you with that, you would be Bless but you could not be a blessing. God wants to Bless us super us super abundantly far over and above infinitely beyond all that we ask or think, beyond our highest prayers, desires, thoughts, hopes or dreams. Read this verse in the Amplified or Message bible as well as K.J.B. I like what the Message bible says about verse 21. Glory to God in the church. Glory to God the Messiah Jesus. Glory down all the generations. Verse 3:20 in

Ephesians, according to the actions of the power that's within us. Remember verse 19 and 20 in Ephesians 1,the exceeding greatness of His power toward us who believe, that mighty power that raise Jesus from the dead, the same power in us. We use by our words. We speak God's words, the promises of God; it's the same as God saying it. It's God's word. You are made in His image and likeness. You have His power in you. Speak it out, declare and decree, make a demand on it, draw that power from you. You create by saying as God did in creation. And you will have success in your life. Now look at 2nd Peter 1:3, 4. God's divine power hath given unto us all things that pertain into life and Godliness. Whereby are given into us exceeding great and precious promises so you can escaped the corruption that the world lust after. In these verses of scriptures I underline, HATH GIVEN and ARE GIVEN. That means these promises are already ours. So we don't have to lust after things like the world does. We just declare and decree.

We call things that be not as though they are according to Romans 4:17. Thats what Abraham the father of faith did, copying his Father God, who is our Heavenly Father, so we should copy our Father and create our success in life. PRAISE THE LORD, give Him Glory. [i am getting emotional] You too, I am sure create, create, create says the Lord. Jesus said in St. Mark 11:23 we could speak to the mountain in our life, with no doubt in our heart and say be removed and we would have what we say. Again P.T.L. [get behind me Satan] James4:7 submit yourselves therefore to God, resist the devil and he will flee from you. The amp. Bible says stand firm against Satan. You are submitting to God doing His word. [now speak it].

CHAPTER 6

Lover Makes It Work

It is all about Love. God is love. 1John 4:8. You will not know God without this love for mankind. To reign and rule with Jesus the motivation must be love. Jesus died for mankind because of God's love. He paid the price for man's sin. So we can be free. Satan has known right to us. He is no longer god of our world. We are back in control, thru Lord Jesus. [P T L] meaning praise the Lord. Since God love us we ought to love one another. 1John4:11 16. God is love and he that dwell in love dwell in God and God in him. We love God because He first loved us. Please read 1John 4:7-21 for yourself. Believe me He loved us first. The good news of Jesus Christ was hid from us. We were lost, because Satan blinded our minds. Because of Adam, Satan became [small g] god of this world system. God [big G] brought us to the light. First in our minds, with the preaching of the gospel, good news of Jesus Christ, got downs in our spirits and we became a new creature. Read 2corinthians 4:3-6 and 2corinthians 5:17. What I am teaching has to be done by faith in your heart. Not just in your heart which is hope. Bible hope has its place. I once preach a message, faith give substance to what you are hoping far. Faith causes what you are hoping far come to pass. You get hope from the word of God. But you must act on that word, far it to become a reality in your life. We are teaching about success in your life. You say what love got to do with it. According to Galatians 5:6 faith work by love. So that's why we have to have a chapter on love before we conclude this book. P T L. The bible is really all about love. God our Father and His love for His children. God made man an exact duplication of Himself. Back to GENESIS1:26,27. The 28 verse said God bless them and the first thing He said to them be fruitful and multiply, or be successful in life. That's love. Here is what the amp. Bible say about this verse. Fill the earth and subdue it, using all its vast resources in the service of God and man. You see from the beginning God provided for man so he could rule in this life and be gods in this world not Satan. Adam could have made him flee using words. He had dominion which is authority to rule. Thank God because of His love we have it all back. Do you see the importance of love. Without the love of God, we would have eternal death instead of eternal life thru His son Lord Jesus Christ. Christ means the anointed one. Through Christ we are anointed ones. So we can reign and rule in life. All because God so love the world. He gave His son so we could have ever lasting life. ST. John3:16. Romans5:5 tell us God's love has been poured in our hearts through the Holy Spirit. So we believers have known excuse not to walk in love. Verse 8 amp bible same chapter says God shows and clearly proves His love for us by the fact that while we were still sinners, Christ died for us. Then we ought to love one another. ST. John13:34,35,the words of Lord Jesus a new commandment I give you that you love one another m as I have love you. By this shall all men know that you are my disciples, if you have love one to another. These verses is very clear, I won't add or take away love one another, God love us, even when we were sinners. I suggest reading St. Luke 6:27-36 and the love chapter 1Corinthians 13. If we applied these chapters into our life, Satan has to flee. You can love like this because the love of God is in the heart of the born again believer. If you are not born again. Pray this prayer; Heavenly

Father I come to you in the name of Jesus.[pray this out loud] Your Word says whosoever shall call on the name of the Lord shall be save and if thou shall confess with the mouth the Lord Jesus and shall believe in thine heart that God has raise Him from the dead, thou shall be save. Romans10:9,10. Acts2:21 [LORD JESUS I confess that you are my LORD and savior I believe in my heart that GOD raise you from the dead. By faith in your word receive salvation now].[i am save, born again. Thank you Jesus.] There's a brand new you". The truth of His word instantly comes to pass in your spirit. Now renew your mind with what I have been teaching you in this book and continue reading your bible, and walking in love. Love never fails. And is the greatest

Conclusion

We are god's small g of course. We must know who we are. Christians as a hold do not know who they are. The unsave has been blinded to who they are. Since many Christians don't know who they are, they can't help the unsaved. The unsaved think we are mere men so does a lot of church people, who say they are Christians. If we study the bible for ourselves and don't just listen to what men say about the bible and get religious ideas, we will get understanding and the revelation of who we are. We are made in His image and likeness, so we are His children. Dogs have dogs, cats have cats. Get the revelation. When we know who we are, we can reign or rule in life, as kings and priests. As king and priests we have authority. Remember Genesis1:28. God bless man and told him to be fruitful and multiply and have dominion which is authority. Kings declare and decree. How and what? [answer words]. Our words must be God's word. Then we create the promises of God in our life. God's word has creative power. Our words have creative power. So we must watch what we say. Remember Proverbs 18:21 death and life are in the power of the tongue. Through test and trials Satan will induce us to say the wrong thing. We must only say what God say. What you look at is also important. Because thoughts get in your heart and affect your words. Thoughts are powerful and effect your imagination. What you see natural has a spiritual effect in your life for success or failure. Remember the tower of Babel in Genesis 11. The power of oneness and imagination. Remember good or bad, success or failure. You have power to use your authority. But it won't work for success in life without LOVE. Remember God is LOVE. Amen, so be it. Love U ed.

THE END

ABOUT THE AUTHOR

Pastor Edward Johnson was save and fill with Holy Spirit in 1966. After serving faithful in Church of God in Christ, he was called to ministry in 1967. And was ordain in 1972. He began pastoring Freedom Temple Church of God in Christ. After hearing the Faith and prosperity massage he began pastoring an independent church. Freedom Miracle Temple. After pastoring for many years God led him to stop and start helping pastors. So he began Freedom Miracle ministries. The vision was a radio ministry, street ministry, working with home, church and other ministries. And last but not least write a book, which he discovered to be his greatest gift and anointing. So be it, my life and legacy. Pastor ED.

NOTES

NOTES

NOTES

Notes

NOTES

NOTES